Cromosys Publication

Teach Yourself French

NIRANJAN JHA SHOWMAN

Founder - Niranjan Jha Showman

Education and Technology Research Center

Patankar Park, Nallasopara (W), Mumbai. +91-9561450045

Education, Technology, Publication, Healthcare, Newsmedia, Realtor, Filmmaking

www.facebook.com/cromosys

+91-9561450045
Learn Advanced Skills
And Get Job Instantly
GERMAN
Python
FRENCH
C++
SPANISH
Java
ENGLISH
HTML5
RUSSIAN
CSS
JavaScript
Cromosys
Education and Technology Research Center
Nallasopara (W), Mumbai

Learn Web Programming
Demo-Class Free
HTML
CSS
React
JavaScript
Typescript
Bootstrap
Cromosys
20 Years of Experience
Nallasopara (W), Mumbai
+91-9561450045

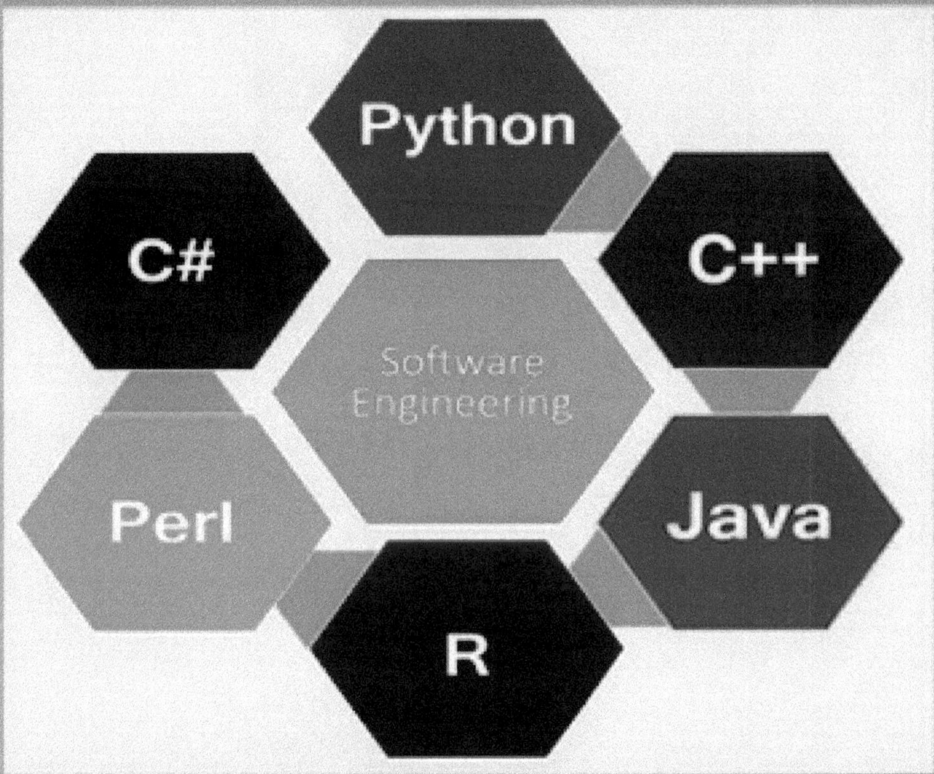

+91-9561450045
Learn Software Engineering
Demo-Class Free
Python
C#
C++
Software
Engineering
Perl
Java
R
Cromosys
20 Years of Experience
Nallasopara (W), Mumbai
+91-9561450045

25 Years of Experience
Learn Visual Multimedia
Animation VFX
Movie Editing
Game Development
Cromosys
+91-9561450045
Education and Technology Research Center
Nallasopara (W), Mumbai
www.facebook.com/cromosys

JoB
Jobs Available
For Candidates Who Know
German
French
Spanish
Vacancy in Germany, France, Spain
For Hospitality, Engineering, IT Sector
With Free Visa, Airfare and Accommodation
Cromosys
Education and Technology Research Centre
Nallasopara (W), Mumbai
+91-9561450045
20 Years of Experience

+91-9561450045

FRANCHISE
Business Offer

Cromosys Publication

Teach Yourself French

Niranjan Jha Showman

"Education taken with zeal educes to success."
~Niranjan Showman

Preface

Cromosys Publication's "Teach Yourself French" book is an optimal quality guide to the beginners as well as advanced learners. French is the language of great demand after English as it is widely spoken in many European countries. Language is the pillar of human origin and evolution, and so, even many other languages of the world died in this century, but French is still surviving and flourishing because of its strong root in human culture and civilization. Moreover, the grammar of French anguage is the base of English grammar too. This book is unmatchable and unique of its kind that guarantees your success. The lessons and study materials exclusively designed are based on my fifteen years of research in linguistic field. The text, audio and video are magnificently powerful to bring you into educational light. Whether your intention is to work, travel abroad or plunge deep into your research, if you need to learn a language, then French is the best choice.

Around eight years ago, when I went to the USA, I got a chance to learn it, and since then I have been teaching this language globally with high exposure. Having been communicating with French-speaking people around the world while managing a team in several call centers, and being able to understand linguistic science, I would like to assure you that this language is easy to learn in just one moth of daily practice. And once learnt, with your sharpened bilingual ability, you can make your way of success without any hindrance. After you start the lesson of this book, you don't need to worry about anything but just follow each and every lesson carefully. Don't procrastinate and never give up. You are going to do the most beautiful thing for yourself, so be bold enough to complete all the lessons. The sentence constructions of French are similar to English, only a few things which are not similar, I have explained properly in the easiest method I could ever find. The pronunciation of each word is given in bracket to help you speak correctly.

The significance of this book is that it is dynamic, systemic and blissful with abundance of pure and perfect set of rules that took a decade of time in preparation. One being immaturely suggested, spends ages in watching movies and listening to the audio in lure of learning French. But it doesn't bring success as they imitate a little but don't learn what in actual sense French is. And their never-ending process of Picasso Adventure collects some scattered information which is unworthy to learning a foreign language. So the aspirants get lost in wilderness. You may have seen some other books on French full of conversations and dialogues which the students purchase by mistake, but they quit learning soon because those are not the proper books. Just memorizing the dialogues will not take you anywhere. So I have designed this book with proper set of lessons to make you start your adventure sitting at home beginning with real basic. This book is highly useful for people working in communication based industry, media houses, entertainment world, and for those who are teachers, writers, researchers and students. And definitely for those who love languages – especially French!

Cromosys, our education and technology research center, saving human efforts from being wasted, is dedicated to teach you this language as good as possible. The world growing with density has brought enormous opportunity to foreign language speakers irrespective of their geographical boundaries. Having been teaching this language from several years, I have come across numerous unique rules which I have elaborated and explained in this book. Our path-breaking pioneer training institute, Cromosys, is committed to enlightening human mind with educational endeavors, and we are doing the same from fifteen successful years. I believe I have done all that I could to make this book useful to you, and not only hopeful but I am sure that your success is in your hand now because this book will take you miles ahead in your expectation. We always respect the views and comments of readers, so for any communication with regards to assistance, enquiry or collaboration, we are always at your reach as it helps us improve our ability.

Niranjan Jha Showman
Trainer, Author, Physician, Entrepreneur, Filmmaker, Activist
Founder of Cromosys Corporation
facebook.com/cromosys
+91-9561450045
cromosys@yahoo.com
Nallasopara (W), Mumbai, India

My other books: -
English Voice Accent and Pronunciation
Teach Yourself German
Teach Yourself French
Teach Yourself Spanish
Be millionaire like me
Dynamic Grammar of English
Teach Yourself HTML5
Teach Yourself 3ds Max
Teach Yourself Autodesk Maya

Cromosys Corporation
Education and Technology Research Center
Education, Technology, Publication, Healthcare, Realtor, Filmmaking
facebook.com/cromosys
+91-9561450045
cromosys@yahoo.com
Nallasopara (W), Mumbai, India

About the Author

Niranjan Jha Showman
Trainer, Author, Physician, Entrepreneur, Filmmaker, Activist

Niranjan Jha Showman is a Language Scientist and Technical Researcher. He is the Award Winning author of more than fifty educational and fictional books at Amazon. He is one of the great-grandsons of the first President of India Dr. Rajendra Prasad. He is a Public Figure, and the globally - renowned Languages Trainer of French, Spanish, and German from past twenty years. Niranjan Jha Showman is an Entrepreneur and also works as a Filmmaker in India. Being the founder and owner of Cromosys Corporation - a company located in Mumbai, India, his company is excelling in the fields of Education, Technology, Publication, Newsmedia, Realtors, Banking, and Cinemascope from past fifteen years.

Niranjan Jha Showman's good-seller educational books and novels are appreciated worldwide. He has more than one million eBook buyers online, and more than one million learners are connected to him globally. One of his novels is critically acclaimed. He is the trainer of French, Spanish, German, English Voice and Accent, and Advanced Computer Education. He is also a political activist in India.

Niranjan Jha Showman is the man who came from rags to riches, he who knows how to turn the table, and he, whom you call the man of Midas-touch. He has observed lives from the Pandora of monkeys to the sanctuary of monks, not only down-to-earth but down-to-grave. He is a B. Com. graduate, and B. Ed. from Delhi University, and diploma holder in French, Spanish and German from America. You can watch his songs, movies, educational videos and many more things by typing "Niranjan Jha Showman" in Google.

Niranjan Jha Showman
+91-9561450045
cromosys@yahoo.com
Mumbai, India
facebook.com/cromosys

Statutory

This book with its content is the registered property of the author Niranjan Jha Showman.
The author and his Cromosys Publication holds all necessary rights of this book.
The copyright certificate of this book is attached at the end of this book.

Lesson 1
Alphabet

There are 26 letters in French alphabet. Next to each letter, the pronunciation, as the name of the letter is given. Write the letter in your notebook and speak out the pronunciation of it for practice. Don't jump to the next lesson without proper practice of this lesson.

A	aa	
B	be	(as 'bay')
C	se	(as 'say')
D	the	(as 'they')
E	oo	(with round lips)
F	ef	
G	zhe	('zhe' as in plea**su**re)
H	aash	
I	ee	
J	zhee	('zhee' as in plea**su**re)
K	kaa	
L	el	
M	em	
N	en	
O	o	
P	pe	(as 'pay')
Q	kyu	
R	er	
S	es	
T	te	(soft - te)
U	iyu	('ee' with round lips)
V	ve	(as 'way')
W	dubl-ve	
X	eeks	
Y	eegrek	
Z	zed	(soft – d)

French is the 6th most spoken language in the world.
The name of letter 'U' is pronounced as 'ee' with round lips.
The letter 'R' coming in a word sounds as guttural voice similar to – H.
More pronunciation hints are given in the next lessons.

Lesson 2
Pronunciation

This lesson explains the proper pronunciation of the letters and lists the examples words with their pronunciation. You are required to concentrate because you may find some pronunciation quite strange. French has a lot of silent letters that makes the pronunciation strange. This lesson lists only those letters which are pronounced differently than English equivalent.

A – It is pronounced as 'aa'.
travail (traavai) = work
jambe (zhaaₙb) = leg

Note- The pronunciation of the word 'jambe' doesn't have a complete 'n' sound in it, but it is a nasal (of nose) sound. And 'zh' is not like 'z' or 'sh' but it is as pronounced in the word 'plea<u>su</u>re' of English, which is a mixed sound of 'z+sh'.

C – It is pronounced like 's'.
This letter is pronounced 's' if it comes before the letters – e, h, i, y. Otherwise it sounds 'k'.
chat (shaa) = cat
casque (kaask) = helmet
cuisine (kweezeen) = food

Note- The word 'chat' is pronounced just 'shaa'. The letter 't' coming at the end, being mute in this word, is not pronounced at all.

E – If this letter comes with Acute Accent like: é, then it is pronounced like a short sound as 'ei' as in the word 'l<u>a</u>te' in English.
cité (seetei) = city
l'Amérique (laameireek) = America

But when this letter is used with Grave Accent like: è, it is pronounced like 'eə' as in 'h<u>air</u>' word of English. It is a combined sound of half 'e' and half 'a'.
père (peər) = father
frère (freər) = brother

This letter is also pronounced 'half a' as in the word 'h<u>er</u>' of English. And in certain words, when it comes at the end, it is completely mute.
cheval (shevaal) = horse
tasse (taas) = cup
mère (meər) = mother
je (zhə) = I

Note – 1. Acute and Grave Accent will be explained in next chapter. 2. The symbol 'ə' used in this book is for pronunciation of 'half a'. 3. French adopted words from Greek, so in altering original pronunciation, many letters were made silent. 4. The word 'casque' is pronounced (kaask) by learner, but (kæsk) by native. Also 'cheval' is (shevaal) by learner, but (shəvaal) by native. 5. Most of the nouns are written in this book with definite 'the' article - l'Amérique = the America. You can bifurcate to understand.

Lesson 3
Pronunciation

G – It is pronounced like 'g' as in 'game' of English only when it comes before- a, o, u or all consonants.
langue (laang) = tongue
figure (feegyur) = face, figure

The word 'langue' has a nasal sound, so 'n' will not be pronounced completely but will go nasal. And from here onwards in this book, wherever you find the letter 'n' in bracket in small size (as laang), make sure you pronounce it nasal.
The word 'figure' has its pronunciation like: feegyur. Yes, no other way!

This letter 'G' in other case is pronounced like 'zh'.
agent (aazhan) = agent
joues (zhoo) = cheeks

The word 'agent' will be pronounced like - 'aazhan' with nasal sound. Don't pronounce like 'aazhan' with complete 'n' sound. In the word 'joues', all the two letters 'es' are silent.

This letter 'G' goes completely silent when it comes before the letter 'n'. For some words, two pronunciations are listed – first is as perfect as native, and second is simply approx okay.
cygne (seeny / seene) = swan
l'Allemagne (laalemaanye / laalemaane) = Germany

'ye' means slight 'e' sound after 'y'.

H – This letter is kept silent.
homme (aum) = man
hanche (aansh) = hip
l'hiver (leever) = winter

I – It sounds like 'ee'.
vide (veed) = empty
Chinois (sheenwaa) = Chinese
il (eel) = he

The letter 'i' also has a short sound also like 'i'.
idiot (eedyo / eediyo) = idiot   (soft 'd')

J – It is pronounced like 'zh' of English.
jeune (zhoen) = young
bonjour (bonzhoor) = good morning, good day
jupe (zhyu-ip) = skirt

It is true that pronunciation is the only difficulty in French, and for that, there is NO HARD AND FAST RULE. Only practicing the sound of each word can help you move step by step ahead. Trust me, there is no other way!
The word 'langue' is pronounced (laang) by learner, but (long) by native.

Lesson 4
Pronunciation

L – It has the same sound as in English.
Lundi (loendi) = Monday
poule (pool) = hen

When 'L' comes at the end of a word, it is not pronounced.
outil (ooti) = tool
détail (detai) = retail

M – It has the same value as in English.
manteau (maanto) = coat
tomate (tawmaat) = tomato

In some words 'M' is pronounced with nasal (of nose) sound.
simple (senpl) = simple
compte (kawnt) = account

N – This letter is pronounced same as in English.
nation (naasyon / naasiyon) = nation
Novembre (novaanbr) = November
poignet (pwaanye) = wrist

When 'N' comes after the letter 'g', the 'g' gets silent and gives 'y' sound.
signal (seenyaal) = signal

In some words 'N' is pronounced with nasal sound.
minion (meenyon) = favorite
grillon (greeyon) = cricket *It is pronounced – gree+aan
chien (shee-aan) = dog

O – It is pronounced like 'aw', but in some words also 'o'.
ordre (awrdr) = order
or (awr) = gold
nom (nawn) = name
dormir (dawrmeer) = to sleep
corps (kawr) = body

If you need to listen to the pronunciation, just type a word in Google Translate or look for a French Talking Dictionary online. Learning French is really a matter of pride because of its strong set of rules. Don't give up, just keep moving.

Pronunciation hints:
'eu' sounds 'half o + half e'. 'oi' sounds 'half a + waa'.
For 'un', 'en', 'im' 'om', 'on' – pronunciation is explained in lesson 10.
For 'corps' the learning pronunciation is (kawr), native sound is (kawh).
You have to ignore too strange native pronunciation.

Lesson 5
Pronunciation

P – It has the same value as in English.
place (plaas) = seat
papier (paapye / paapiye) = paper

If 'P' occurs at the end of a word, or it is preceded by 'm', the letter 'p' remains silent.
drap (draa) = sheet
temps (taan) = time   *It is not 'taan' or 'temps'.

Q – It has the same value as in English.
quand (kaan) = when
question (kestyon / kestiyon) = question

R – This letter is pronounced same as in English.
Paris (paaree) = Paris
rapport (raapawr) = report

But the ending 'R' remains mute.
changer (shaanzhe) = to change
banquier (baankye / baankiye) = banker

S – If it comes in the beginning or middle of a word, it is pronounced same as in English.
sabre (saabr) = sword
si (see) = if
dentiste (daanteest) = dentist

If 'S' occurs at the end of a word, it is not pronounced.
pansements (paansemaan) = bandages
vagues (vaag) = waves

The letter 'S' sounds like 'z' when it comes between two vowels.
chaise (shez) = chair
troisième (trwaazi-em) = third

T – It is not pronounced as in English. Instead of hard, it is a soft sound.
citron (seetron) = lemon
poitrine (pwaatreen) = chest

Ending 'T' of a word remains silent.
doigt (dwaa) = finger
lait (lai) = milk

'pansements' is pronounced (paansemaan), but correct sound is (paansmaan) as **Vowel Swift**.
'question' has (kestyon) as perfect sound, but (kestiyon) is **Simply Approx**.
'corps' is pronounced (kawr), but sounding (kawh) is **Native Pronunciation**.
Google Translate, Wiktionary, and Collions online dictionary can help you in pronunciation.

Lesson 6
Pronunciation

U – This letter has 'iyu' sound in French.
futur (fyutyur) = future
uniforme (iyunee-fawrm) = uniform

If 'U' comes before 'm' or 'n', it sounds like 'oeɳ'.
parfum (paarfoeɳ) = perfume

V – It has the same value as in English.
vache (vaash) = cow
valise (vaaleez) = suitcase

W – It is pronounced like 'v' and also 'w' as in English.
wagon (vaagawɳ) = wagon
whisky (veeskee) = whisky

X – It is pronounced same as in English.
excuse (ekskyuz) = excuse

In some words 'X' is pronounced like 's'.
six (sees) = six
dix (dees) = ten

The ending 'X' is always silent.
cheveux (shevu / shəvu) = hair
deux (du) = two

Y – It is pronounced like 'ee'.
yeux (yu) = eyes
polygone (poleegon) = polygon

Z – This letter is pronounced same as in English.
zéro (zero) = zero
zodiaque (zawdyaak / zawdiyaak) = zodiac

At the end of a word 'Z' is generally silent.
nez (ne) = nose
arrêtez (aaretay) = stop

In 'cheveux' the pronunciation (shevu) has 'u' as – round lips 'u'.
Pronouncing 'cheveux' as (shəvu) is because of **Vowel Shift**.
In 'parfum' the part 'um' sounds (oeɳ) that is explained later.
The sound 'o' and 'aw' are near to each other in French.
The sound 'e' and 'ei' are near to each other in French.

Strict Instructions

Remember that learning French is never difficult. The only thing you have to do is that take this book as a guide to lead you step by step. Till now, you have completed six lessons. Things are easy but get more logical and logical as you move ahead. For that, it requires proper practice by writing the lesson from this book into your notebook and practicing the pronunciation of the words. If you ignore and do not do this, things from here will get difficult. So before moving ahead, make sure you have done proper practice from beginning till sixth lesson.

Just looking into this book, with pleasure seeking attitude, can make you laugh a little as you see French words, but if you are really interested to learn it, then be serious about it. Don't jump off and scroll down to other pages without having a proper practice done on all the previous lessons. Why it is necessary is that while learning a foreign language, even your single slip will take you to the bottom from where you can't even think of starting back again. If English is your first language, imagine how the other people learn! I can tell you, English is also not easy to billions of people of the world. Some people learn it after great effort and putting everything on stake.

In the same way, you have to put efforts to learn this language. You won't learn it automatically, because if it were easy, you would not buy this book. You would have learnt it by yourself. There are many people who want to learn a new language because it helps them in career, but many of them fail in the beginning only because they don't practice. For them, grapes are sour!

What is easy in the world? And if something is easy, what benefit the easy thing can give you? Nothing. If you want great success, you have to do great work – hard work. Remember that only difficult thing brings amazing success in your life. So refrain yourself from behaving like a playboy learner and be a little serious about it.

(1) You can enjoy the world of French only after you completely go through this book.
(2) Daily practices in reading, writing, speaking and listening is mendatory.
(3) Doing excercises is always beneficial to evaluate yourself.
(4) Once you are thorough, you may need to buy a French-to-English dictionary.
(5) You may watch some audio-video conversation online.
(6) Google Translate will help you tremendously for your all need.
(7) If you get a chance to talk with native French, it will be fabulous.

Wishing you all the best! Don't quit, continue learning.

Lesson 7
The Accent Marks
The Accent Marks are of six types and they are placed over mostly the vowels – a, e, u.

The Acute Accent
It is called L'accent aigu (laaksan tegyu) in French. It comes only on 'e' as – é, which is pronounced like (ei) or (e).
été (eitei) = summer
café (kaafei) = coffee

The Grave Accent
It is called L'aacent grave (laaksan graav). It occurs as è, à, ù – to be pronounced (eə), (aa), (oo).
père (peər) = father
voilà (vwaalaa) there is
où (oo) = where

The Circumflex Accent
The L'accent circonflexe (laaksan sirkonflex) may occur over any vowel accept semi-vowel 'y'. It indicates the omission of 's' sound from the word concerned.
forêt (fawre) = forest
hôte (ot) = host

La Cèdilla
La Cèdille (laa sediye) is placed under the letter c, like – ç when it comes before the letters a, o, u. The letter 'c' accompanied with Cèdille mark sounds 's' not 'k' in French.
garçon (gaarson) = boy
français (fraanse / fronse) = French
leçons (leson) = lessons
reçu (resyu) = received

Le Trema
Le Trema (Lə tremaa) looks like (¨) which is placed on second vowel in certain words where there are two vowels together. The vowel having this mark is pronounced separately from the one coming before.
ciguë (seegyui) = hemlock tree
In this word 'ë' is pronounced like slight 'i' separately.
If there were no trema on 'e' and the word was written like 'cigue', then it would be pronounced (seeg) because 'e' would go mute.

L'apostrophe
L'apostrophe (laapawstrawf) is like apostrophe (') of English. This mark indicates that a vowel has been removed from that place.
l'heure (lo-er) = the hour
The full value of the word (l'heure) is – la heure which is shortened in writing.

The letter 'eu' is pronounced (oe) and also (round u).
The word été is pronounced (eitei), but **Simply Approx** (ete).
The word français is pronounced (fronse) as **Native Pronunciation**.

Lesson 8
Final Consonants

In French, the last consonant of a word is usually silent.
petit (petee) = small, tiny, slim, young
doux (doo) = soft
souris (sooree) = mouse
riz (ree) = rice
avis (aavee) = notice

However there are certain final consonants which retain their sounds. The final consonants which retain their sounds are – c, f, l, r.
chef (shef) = chief
il (eel) = he
boeuf (boef) = beef
jour (zhoor) = day
coeur (koer) = heart

The letter 'r' is silent in most of the multi-syllable words which end with 'er'.
parler (paarle) = to speak
lever (leve) = to lift
Février (fevreeye) = February
demander (demaande) = to request
collier (kawleeye) = necklace

In French, most of the words end with vowel letters.
regrette (regret) = regret   (verb form of I)
classe (klaas) = class
poule (pool) = hen
rouge (roozh) = red
peigne (penye) = comb

Some words with their pronunciation.
gigot (zheego) = leg of lamb
col (kawl) = collar
bouton (bootawn) = button
cousin (koozen) = cousin
pomme (pawm) = apple

The word 'coeur' is pronounced (keər) as Native Pronunciation.
The ending 'r' in all French verbs remain silent.

Lesson 9
Capital letters

The capital letters are not used as frequently as in English.
It is used in following cases:-

First and last name begins with a capital letter.
Jaque Souniér
William Martinez

Geographical name begins with a capital letter.
l'Amérique (laamereek) = America

Personifications start with capital.
la République (laa repyubleek) = the republic

A capital letter is used in the starting of monuments' name.
l'Opéra (lawpera) = opera

The first letter of a word beginning with a sentence is kept capital.
Comment allez-vous? (kawmaaₙ taale voo) = How are you?

Capitals are not used in following cases:-

The pronouns start with a small letter.
je suis. (zhə swee) = I am.

The name of the days begins with a small letter.
mardi (maardee) = Tuesday

The name of the months starts with a small letter.
janvier (zhaaₙviye) = January

The nationality is written starting with a small letter.
anglais (aaₙglai) = English

The title before a person's name is written starting with a small letter.
Voici monsieur Smith (vwaasee moₙsyu) = Here is Mr. Smith.

Hints:-
Comment allez – pronunciation (kawmaaₙ taale) is called **Interconnect Pronunciation**.
The word monsieur, after **Vowel Swift**, is also pronounced (mənsyu).
'ui' = (uwi) and (ee) – nui (nwee) = night; qui (kee) = who.
'y' used in this book as pronunciation is near to 'i' or 'e'.
's' is pronounced (z) when it comes between two vowels.
'eu' or 'eux' is pronounced as (round 'u').
'ou' should be pronounced as (oo).

Lesson 10
Nasal sounds

The letters 'm' and 'n' have nasal sounds coming from nose. The nasal sound takes place when these letters are preceded by vowels in the same syllable, like – an, am, em, aon.

1. an, am, en, em, sound like (aan).
tante (taant) = aunt
blanc (blaan) = white
bien (byaan / biyaan) = well
combien (konbyaan) = how many
chambre (shaanbr) = room

2. on, om, aon, are pronounced like (awn).
sont (sawn) = are
commencer (kawmaanse) = to begin

3. in, im, ain, aim, ym, ein, lin, lim sound like (en).
faim (fen) = hungry
timbres (tenbr) = stamps
main (men) = hand
pain (pen) = bread
sein (sen) = breast

4. un, um, eum sound like (oen).
lundi (loendee) = Monday
brun (broen) = brown

5. ille is pronounced (eeye).
fille (feeye) = girl
famille (faameeye) = family

Punctuation marks
le point (lə pwaan) = full point (.)
la virgule (laa veergyul) = comma (,)
le trait d'union (lə trai dyunyon) = hyphen (-)
le point virgule (lə pwaan veergyul) = semicolon (;)
les deux point (le du pwaan) = colon (:)
le point d'interrogation (dentero-gaasyon) = question mark (?)

For 'colon' there is one more meaning as – côlon (kolawn).
'ou' is pronounced (oo) – jour (zhoor) = day, poumon (poomawn) = lung.
'i' is pronounced (ee) – fils (fees) = son, visage (veezaazh) = face.
'ui' is pronounced (uwi) – huit (uweet) = eight, cuisse (kwees) = thigh.
'un' is pronounced much compressed (oen), which may also sound (ən).

Lesson 11
Articles

The noun must come with an article in French. The articles are – un, une, le, la

un – (ən) is a masculine indefinite article like 'a' of English.
une – (iyun) is a feminine indefinite article like 'a' of English.
le – (lə) is a masculine definite article like 'the' of English.
la – (laa) is a feminine definite article like 'the' of English.

un (ən) or (en) is used before a masculine singular noun. It is pronounced (ən) not (~~un~~). It is a mixed sound of 'ə' + nasal 'n'.

un garçon (ən gaarsawn) = a boy
un livre (ən leevr) = a book
un chapeau (ən shaapo) = a hat
un citron (ən seetron) = a lemon
un homme (ən + om = ənawm) = a man   *Because of vowel contraction 'n' gives full sound*

Notable points: -
In French, all nonliving things like hat, lemon are also categorized either masculine or feminine gender. In the word 'un homme' as second word 'homme' starts with a vowel sound because 'h' is mute, so both words get connected in pronunciation. And it is pronounced (ənom) with full sound and no nasal of letter 'n'. It can't be (~~ain om~~).

une (iyun) comes before a feminine singular noun.
It's sound is (i+yu+n).

une fille (iyun feeye) = a girl
une soeur (iyun soyer) = a sister
une femme (iyun faam) = a woman or wife
une mouche (iyun mosh) = a fly
une ceinture (iyun sentyur) = a belt

Notable points: -
In the word 'fille' the 'll' is mute, so it is pronounced (feeye or fee-e) with a little separate 'e' sound.
The word 'ceinture' is pronounced (sen + tyu + r).

le (lə) is used before a masculine singular noun.
It is pronounced just (l + half a) not (~~le~~).

le garçon (lə gaarson) = the boy
le mari (lə maaree) = the husband
le fils (lə fees) = the son
le gâteau (lə gaato) = the cake
le jupon (lə zhyupon) = the petticoat

<u>Notable points</u>: -
There is no fixed rule to categorize masculine and feminine words. It should be memorized.

la (laa) is used before a feminine singular noun.

la fille (laa feeye) = the daughter or girl
la nièce (laa nyes) = the niece
la jupe (laa zhyup) = the skirt
la glace (laa glaas) = the ice
le thé (lə te) = the tea

Exercise:-
Write down the meaning of these words in French and practice the pronunciation correctly.
name
paper
breast
small
soft
notice
body
boy
French
hair

Write down the meaning of these words in English and practice the French pronunciation correctly.
souris
riz
main
gigot
col
bouton
laçons
reçu
cousin
pomme

Pronuncation challenges:-
Vowel Swift
Simply Approx
Native Pronunciation
Interconnect Pronunciation
Unreasonable Simplification

Pronunciation is a major concern in French. In every French-to-English dictionary, the pronunciation and gender of each word is written. So, it can help you a lot. If you still find any difficulty, try to search for the pronunciation by typing the word in Google Translate, or download a French dictionary.

Lesson 12
Contraction of article

When a masculine or feminine noun is plural, le or la is changed into 'les'.

les (le / lay) is used before a plural noun. It is pronounced (le or lay) not (~~les~~).
The following list makes everything clear about article.

un garçon (ən gaarson) = a boy
une fille (iyun feeye) = a girl
le garçon (lə gaarson) = the boy
la fille (laa feeye) = the girl
les garçons (lay gaarson) = the boys
les filles (lay feeye) = the girls

Notable points: -
Most of the nouns take 's' at the end in plural form. You will be explained in detail in next lessons.
The ending 's' of a plural noun is mute.
For both masculine and feminine plural noun, the definite article 'les' is used.

un homme (anawm) = a man
une femme (iyun faam) = a woman
l'homme (lawm) = the man   (le + home)
la femme (laa faam) = the woman
les hommes (lezawm) = the men
les femmes (lay faam) = the women

Notable points: -
Because of vowel contraction between two words, 'le homme' is pronounced (lawm), not (~~ley om~~). In
'les hommes' the ending 's' of 'les' is pronounced like 'z' because next word starts with a vowel sound.

un père (ən peər) = a father
une mère (iyun meər) = a mother
le père (lə peər) = the father
la mère (laa meər) = the mother
les pères (lay peər) = the fathers
les mères (lay meər) = the mothers

un ami (ənaami) = a boyfriend
une amie (iyunaamee) = a girlfriend
l'ami (laamee) = the boyfriend
l'amie (laamee) = the girlfriend
les amis (lezaamee) = the boyfriends
les amies (lezaamee) = the girlfriends

Note: - If one word ends with a vowel letter and next word starts with another vowel letter, they both
are contracted. So le + ami will be written as l'ami. Most of the nouns in this book are written with
definite 'the' article as per French. You can bifurcate them to understand.

Lesson 13
Singular – Plural Noun

The rules: -
1. The plural is generally formed by adding 's' at the end of a word, and the 's' is not pronounced.
la chaise (laa shaiz) = the chair
les chaises (lay shaiz) = the chairs
l'enfant (laanfaan) = the child
les enfants (lezaanfaan) = the children

2. If the singular already has an 's' at the end, then it doesn't undergo any change.
le corps (laa kawr) = the body
les corps (lay kawr) = the bodies
le fils (lə fees) = the son
les fils (lay fees) = the sons
le mois (lə mwaa) = the month
les mois (lay mwaa) = the months
la brebis (laa brebee) = the sheep
les brebis (lay brebee) = the many sheep

3. If the nouns end with the letter 'x' or 'z', they don't undergo any change.
le prix (lə pree) = the price
les prix (lay pree) = the prices
le nez (lə ne) = the nose
les nez (lay ne) = the noses

4. The nouns ending in 'al' or 'ail' replace them with 'aux'.
le cheval (lə shevaal) = the horse
les chevaux (lay shevo) = the horses
le travail (lə tvaavai) = the work
les travaux (lay tvaavo) = the works
l'animal (laaneemaal) = the animal
les animaux (lezaaneemo) = the animals

5. The nouns ending in eu, au, eau, ou take 'x' and the end. There are some exceptions also.
le neveu ((lə nevu) = the nephew *It can be pronounced 'neve' or 'neyvey'
les neveux (lay nevu) = the nephews
un oiseau (ənwaazo) = a bird   oiseau (waazo)
les oiseaux (lezwaazo) = the birds
un bureau (ən byuro) = an office
les bureaux (ley byuro) = the offices

Note: - There are some exceptions to these rules. Some nouns do not follow any rule.
'aux' is pronounced (o), and 'eux' at the end is (round 'u'), but 'eux' in the middle (oe).

Lesson 14
Gender

There is no neuter gender in French. Almost all nouns ending in a mute 'e' are feminine except those ending in isme, age, and iste. There are some exceptions to this.
Almost all nouns ending in a consonant or a vowel other than mute 'e' are masculine except those ending in ion and té. There are some exceptions to this.

<u>Changing gender</u>

1. The feminine is formed by adding the letter 'e' at the end of a masculine word. In some cases, the pronunciation in both of genders remains same, only articles le and la distinguish them in speaking.
le cousin (lə koozen) = cousin brother
la cousine (laa koozeen) = cousin sister
ami (aamee) = boyfriend
amie (aamee) = girlfriend

2. The masculine nouns ending in 'er' form their feminine changing it to ère.
laitier (letiye) = milkman
laitière (letiyer) = milk-woman
boulanger (boolaanzhe) = male-baker
boulangère (boolaanzher) = female-baker

3. Some nouns ending in -an, -en, -on form their feminine by replacing them with –anne, –enne –onne.
paysan (peizaan) = male farmer
paysanne (peizaan) = female farmer
lion (lyon) = lion
lionne (lyon) = lioness

4. Masculine nouns ending in –p or –f change their letter into 've'.
loup (loo) = wolf
louve (loov) = femal wolf

5. Masculine nouns ending in –eur form their feminine in –euse.
vendeur (vaandoer) = salesman
vendeuse (vaanduz) = saleswoman   (round 'u')
chanteur (shaantoer) = male singer
chanteuse (shaantuz) = female singer   (round 'u')

6. Masculine nouns ending in –eux or –oux form their feminine in –euse, –ouse.
époux (eipoo) = male spouse
épouse (eipooz) = female spouse

7. Most masculine words ending in –e change in –esse.
prince (prens) = prince
princesse (prenses) = princess

Note: - There are some exceptions to all these rules.

Lesson 15
Forming sentences with Adjective

An adjective in French must agree with the gender and number of the noun or pronoun.

Rule 1
petit (petee) = little
little (masculine singular) = petit (petee)
little (masculine plural) = petits (petee)
little (feminine singular) = petite (peteet)
little (feminine plural) = petites (peteet)

Note: - The adjective changes according to the gender and number of a noun or pronoun. But the pronunciation remains same. The feminine adjective is made by adding –e to the masculine.
Examples:-
the little boy = le petit garçon. (lə petee gaarsawn)
the little boys = les petits garçons. (lay petee gaarson)
the little girl = la petite fille. (laa peteet feeye)
the little girls = les petites filles. (lay petete feeye)

grand (graan) = tall
the tall man = le grand homme. (lə graan dawm)
the tall men = les grands hommes. (lay graan zawm)
the tall woman = la grande femme. (laa graand faam)
the tall women = les grandes femmes. (lay graand faam)

Masculine		Feminine
joli (zhawlee)	= pretty	jolie (zhawlee)
jeune (zhoen)	= young	jeune (zhoen)
intelligent (enteleezhaan) = intelligent		intelligente (enteleezhaant)
élégant (elegaan)	=tasteful	élégante (elegaant)

Rule 2
The masculine adjectives ending in –f changes into –v while making them feminine.

Masculine		Feminine
vif (veef)	= lively / bright	vive (veev)
bref (bref)	= short	brève (brev)
neuf (noef)	= new	neuve (noev)

Rule 3
The masculine adjectives ending in –x changes into –se while making them feminine.

Masculine		Feminine
jaloux (zhaaloo)	= jealous	jalouse (zhaalooz)
heureux (uru)	= happy	heureuse (uruz)
paresseux (paaresu)	= lazy	paresseuse (paaresuz)

Rule 4

The adjectives ending in –er or –ier changes into –ère or –ière while making them feminine.

Masculine	Feminine
cher (sher) = expensive	chère (sheər)
léger (lezhe) = lightweight	légère (lezheər)
premier (premiye) = first	première (premiyer)
dernier (derniye) = last	dernière (derniyer)
amer (aamer) = bitter	amère (aameər)
familier (faameeliye) = familiar	familière (faameeliyeər)

Rule 5

The adjectives ending in –gu form their feminine by adding an 'e' with tréma.

Masculine	Feminine
long (lawn) = long	longuë (lawng)
aigu (egyu) = acute	aiguë (egyui)

Some irregular adjectives-

gentil (zhantee) = nice, gentle	gentille (zhanteeye)
bon (bawn) = good	bonne (bon) *Full 'n' sound*
ancien (aansiyen)= old	ancienne (aansiyen)
cruel (kri-yu-el) = cruel	cruelle (kri-yu-el)
las (laa) = tired	lasse (laas)
gros (gro) = big	grosse (gros)
net (net) = clean	nette (net)
sot (so) = foolish	sotte (sot)

Exercise:-

Translate these sentences into French.

The happy prince
The dear princess
The young cousin-brother
The pretty cousin-sister
The intelligent salesman
The new saleswoman
The old male-farmer
The tall female-farmer

'eu' has three pronunciation – 1. (iyu), 2. (oe), 3. (round 'u').
eu (iyu) = had; neuf (noef) = new; feu (fu) = fire.

I know how tough it is, but, remember only tough thing give you great success.

Lesson 16
Forming sentences with Preposition

à (aa) = to or at
de (də) = of or from   (soft 'd')

When these prepositions come along the articles 'le', they undergo a change.
to the boy = au garçon (à+le = au – pronounced 'o')
at the boy = au garçon
of the boy = du garçon (de+le = du – pronounced 'dyu')
from the boy = du garçon
to the boys = aux garçons (à+les = aux – pronounced 'o')
to a boy = à un garçon (No change)

But in case of 'la', there is no change.
to the girl = à la fille (No change)
of the girl = de la fille (No change)
to the girls = aux filles (aux – pronounced 'o')
of the girls = des filles (des – pronounced 'de')
to a girl = à une fille (No change)

When the noun associated with the preposition stats with a vowel sound, there is no change.
to the man = à l'homme
of the man = de l'homme
to a man = à un homme (aa anawm)
of a man = d'un homme (d'un = de+un) (doe nawm)

Exercise:-
Translate these sentences into French.

To the father
At the father
Of the father
From the father
To the fathers
To a father

To the mother
Of the mother
To the mothers
To a mother

Lesson 17
Days, Months and Seasons

The days = les jours (lay zhoor)
Sunday	Dimanche (deemaansh)
Monday	Lundi (loendee)
Tuesday	Mardi (maardee)
Wednesday	Mercredi (merkredee)
Thursday	Jeudi (zhudee)
Friday	Vendredi (vaandredee)
Saturday	Samedi (saamdee)

The months = les mois (lay mwaa)
January	Janvier (zhaanveeye)
February	Février (fevreeye)
March	Mars (maars)
April	Avril (aavreel)
May	Mai (me / may)
June	Juin (zhwee-en)
July	Juillet (zhwee-ye)
August	Août (oot)
September	Septembre (septaanbr)
October	Octobre (awktawbr)
November	Novembre (novaanbr)
December	Décembre (desaanbr)

The seasons = les saisons (lay sezawn)
spring	le printemps (lə prentaan)
summer	l'été (leitei / lete)
autumn	l'automne (lawtawn)
winter	l'hiver (leever)

Time = le temps (taan)
today	aujourd'hui (ozhoor-dwi)
tomorrow	demain (demen)
day after tomorrow	après demain (aapre demen)
yesterday	hier (ee-yer / ee-er)
day before yesterday	avant hier (aavaan teeyer)
tonight	ce soir (sə swaar)
night	nuit (nwi)
morning	matin (maaten)
afternoon	l'après midi (laapre meedee)
evening	soirée (swaare)

The word 'hier' is pronounced (ee-er), but it is written in this book as (ee-yer).

Lesson 18
Number = nombre (nonbr)

one	un (ən)
two	deux (du)
three	trois (trwaa)
four	quatre (kaatr)
five	cinq (sɛnk)
six	six (sees)
seven	sept (set)
eight	huit (uweet)
nine	neuf (noef)
ten	dix (dees)
eleven	onze (awnz)
twelve	douze (dooz)
thirteen	treize (trez)
fourteen	quatorze (kaatawrz)
fifteen	quinze (kɛnz)
sixteen	seize (sez)
seventeen	dix-sept (deeset)
eighteen	dix-huit (deezweet)
nineteen	dix-neuf (deeznoef)
twenty	vingt (vɛn)
twenty-one	vingt et un (vɛn teən) *et (e) = and*
twenty-two	vingt deux (vɛn du)
thirty	trente (traant)
forty	quarante (kaaraant)
fifty	cinquante (sɛnkaant)
sixty	soixante (swaasaant)
seventy	soixante-dix (swaasaant dees)
eighty	quatre vingt (kaatr vɛn)
ninety	quatre vingt dix (kaatr vɛn dees)
one hundred	cent (saan)
one thousand	mille (meel)
one million	un million (ən meelyawn)
first	premier (premeeye)
second	deuxième (duziyem)
third	troisième (trwaaziyem)
fourth	quatrième (kaatriyem)
fifth	cinquième (sɛnkiyem)
sixth	sixième (seeziyem)
seventh	septième (setiyem)
eighth	huitième (uweetiyem)
ninth	neuvième (noeviyem)
tenth	dixième (deeziyem)

'vingt-et-un' is pronounced (vɛn te-ən) as **Unreasonable Simplification**.

Lesson 19
Family = la famille (faameeye)

father	le père (peər)
mother	la mère (meər)
parents	les parents (paaraan)
grandfather	le grand-père (graan peər)
grandmother	la grand-mère
son	le fils (fees)
daughter	la fille (feeye)
granddaughter	la petite-fille
grandson	le petit-fils
brother	le frère (freər)
sister	la soeur (soyer)
uncle	l'oncle (lawnkl)
aunt	la tante (taant)
nephew	le neveu (nevu)
niece	la nièce (nyes)
husband	le mari (maaree)
wife	la femme (faam)
father-in-law	le beau-père (bo peər)
mother-in-law	la belle-mère (bel meər)
son-in-law	le beau-fils
daughter-in-law	la belle-fille
child	l'enfant (laanfaan)
boyfriend	l'ami (aamee)
girlfriend	l'amie (aamee)
bachelor	le célibataire (seleebaater)
relationship	relation (relaasyon)
marriage	le mariage (maaryaazh)
fiancé	le fiancé (fyaanse)
fiancée	la fiancée (fyaanse)
stepfather	le beau-père
stepbrother	le beau-frère
stepdaughter	la belle-fille
stepmother	la belle- mère
relative	relatif (relaateef)
neighbor	voisin (vwaazen)
married	marié (maariye)
lover	lamant.(aamaan)
friendship	amitié (aameetiye)
love	le amour (aamoor)
classmate	camarade de classe (kaamaaraad də klass)
colleague	collègue (kawleg)

Lesson 20
Body = le corps (kawr)

head	la tête (tet)
hair	les cheveux (shevu)
face	le visage (veezaazh)
eyes	les yeux (lezyu)
forehead	le front (fraan)
eyebrows	les sourcils (soorsee)
eye lashes	les cils (seel)
moustache	la moustache (moostash)
mouth	le bouche (boosh)
lips	les lèvres (levr)
tongue	la langue (laang)
teeth	les dents (daan)
gums	les gencives (zhaanseev)
cheeks	les joues (zhoo)
ears	les oreilles (awre - lezawre)
chin	le menton (maantawn)
beard	la barbe (baarb)
throat	la gorge (gawrzh)
neck	le cou (koo)
shoulder	les épaules (epol)
back	le dos (doh)
chest	la poitrine (pwaatreen)
breasts	les seins (sen)
arms	les bras (braa)
elbow	le coude (kood)
wrist	le poignet (pwaanye)
hand	la main (men)
finger	le doigt (dwaa)
nails	les ongles (awngl - lezawngl)
heart	le coeur (koer)
lung	le poumon (poomawn)
liver	le foie (fwaa)
stomach	le ventre (vaantr)
thigh	la cuisse (kwees)
hip	la hanche (aansh - laansh)
knee	le genou (zhenoo)
leg	la jambe (zhaanb)
foot	le pied (pye)
skull	le crâne (kraan)
brain	le cerveau (servo)

'eu' sounds (oe) – coeur (koer) = heart.
'au' sounds (o) – jaune (zhon) = yellow.
'oe' sounds (oe) – oeil (oe) = eye.

Lesson 21
Food = la nourriture (nooreetyur)

milk	le lait (lai)
cake	le gâteau (gaato)
cheese	le fromage (frawmaazh)
butter	le beurre (boer)
rice	le riz (ree)
omelet	l'omelette (awmlet - lawmlet)
egg	l'oeuf (oef - loef)
tea	la thé (te)
coffee	le café (kaafe)
water	l'eau (o - lo)
chocolate	le chocolat (shawkawla)
beef	le boeuf (boef)
pork	le porc (pawr)
sugar	le sucre (syukr)
salt	le sel (sel)
pepper	le poivre (pwaavr)
bread	le pain (peₙ)
meat	la viande (vyaaₙd)
wine	le vin (veₙ)
beer	la bière (byer)
onion	l'oignon (awnyawₙ)
carrots	la carotte (kaarawt)
beans	les haricots (aareeko - lezaareeko)
cabbage	le chou (shoo)
cauliflower	le choufleur (shoo floer)
cucumber	le concombre (kawₙkawₙbr)
tomato	la tomate (tawmaat)
potato	la patate (paataat)
garlic	l'ail (aay - laay)
melon	le melon (melawₙ)
apple	la pomme (pom)
orange	l'orange (awraaₙzh)
grapes	les raisins (rezeₙ)
cherries	les cerises (sereez)
lemon	le citron (seetrawₙ)
wheat	le blé (ble)
ice	la glace (glaas)
lunch	le déjeuner (dezhoene)
dinner	le dîner (deene)
breakfast	le petit déjeuner (dezhoene)

For potato = la patate (paataat) or le pomme de terre (pom də ter).
For native 'r' in the beginning, or between two vowels, sounds normal 'r' – ~~not 'h'~~.
But in other case, for native, 'r' sounds as guttural voice – H.

Lesson 22
Work = travail (traavai)

company	le société (sawsyete)
balance	la balance (baalaans)
credit	le crédit (kredee)
debit	le débit (debee)
partnership	l'association (aasosaasyoon)
partner	l'associé (aasosye)
clerk	le commis (kawmi)
receipt	l'acquit (aakee)
debt	la dette (det)
debtor	le débiteur (debeetoyer)
creditor	le créancier (kre-aan-sye)
bill	le billet (beeye)
invoice	la facture (faaktyur)
cashier	le caissier (kesye)
banker	le banquier (baankye)
trader	le négociant (negawsyaan)
account	le compte (kawnt)
retail	le détail (detai)
order	le mandat (maandaa)
sale	le vente (vaant)
rate	le taux (toh)
sample	l'échantillon (eshaan-tee-on)
reduction	le rabais (raabe)
change	le change (shaanzh)
balance-sheet	le bilan (beelaan)
correspondence	la correspondence (kawrespondaans)
notice	le avis (aavee)
office	le bureau (byuro)
discount	l'escompte (eskawnt)
retailer	détaillant (detai-aan)
cost	coût (koo)
total	total (tawtaal)
loss	la perte (pert)
profit	le profit (prawfee)
income	la revenu (revenyu)
letter	la lettre (letr)
date	la date (daat)
paper	le papier (paapye)
ink	l'encre (aankr)
envelop	l'enveloppe (aanvelawp)
stamp	le timbre-poste (tenbr pawst)
registered	recommandé (rekawmaande)

Lesson 23
Clothes = vêtements (vetemaan)

shirt	la chemise (shemeez)
trouser	le pantalon (paantaalon)
coat	le veston (vestaan)
overcoat	le pardessus (paardesyu)
hat	le chapeau (shaapo)
tie	la cravate (kraavaat)
cap	la casquette (kaasket)
shoes	les chaussures (shosyur)
belt	la ceinture (sentyur)
collar	le col (kawl)
suit	le vêtement (vetemaan)
gloves	les gants (gaan)
vest	le gilet (zheele)
hand tie	les manchetes (maanshet)
button	le bouton (bootawn)
handkerchief	le mouchoir (mooshwaar)
blouse	la chemisette (shemeezet)
skirt	la jupe (zhyup)
bra	le soutien-gorge (sootyen-gawrzh)
petticoat	le jupon (zhyupon)
necklace	le collier (kawlye)
earrings	les boucles d'oreille (bookl dawre)
comb	le peigne (penye)
bikini	bikini (beekeenee)
ring	la bague (baag)
powder	la poudre (poodr)
cream	la crème (krem)
towel	la serviette (servyet)
shoelace	le lacet (laase)

Color = la couleur (kooloyer)

red	rouge (roozh)
pink	rosé (roze)
white	blanc (blaan)
blue	bleu (blu)
brown	brun (bro-en)
green	vert (ver)
yellow	jaune (zhon)
gray	gris (gree)
black	noir (nwaar)

Lesson 24
Animal = l'animal (aaneemaal)

cow	la vache (vaash)
horse	le cheval (shevaal)
ox	le boeuf (boef)
dog	le chien (shyaan)
cat	le chat (shaa)
lamb	la gigot (zheego)
sheep	la brebis (brebee)
pig	le porc (pawr)
goat	la chèvre (shevr)
donkey	l'ane (aan)
tiger	le tigre (teegr)
rat	le rat (raa)
mouse	le singe (senzh)
duck	le canard (kaanaar)
cock	le coq (kawk)
chicken	le poulet (poole)
hen	la poule (pool)
pigeon	le pigeon (peezhawn)
partridge	la perdrix (perdree)
canary	le serin (seren)
eagle	l'aigle (egl)
lion	lion (lyon)
bull	le taureau (tawro)
kangaroo	la kangourou (kaangooroo)
penguin	le pingouin (pengwen)
buffalo	le bison (beezawn)
fox	la renard (renaar)
ant	la fourmi (foormee)
fly	la mouche (moosh)
mosquito	le moustique (moosteek)
caterpillar	la chenille (shenee-ye)
worm	le vers (ver)
snail	l'escargot (eskaargo)
cobra	le cobra (kawbraa)
crocodile	le crocodile (krawkawdeel)
frog	la grenouille (grenu-ye)
snake	le serpent (serpaan)
spider	l'araignée (aarenye)
moth	la mite (meet)

Lesson 25
Country = le pays (pe)

China	la Chine (sheen)
Germany	l'Allemagne (aalemaanye)
America	l'Amérique (aamereek)
England	l'Angleterre (angleter)
Switzerland	la Suisse (swees)
Russia	la Russie (ryusee)
Japan	le Japon (zhaapawn)
Spain	l'Espagne (espaanye)
Greece	la Grèce (gres)
India	l'Inde (end / lend)
France	le France (fraans)
Ireland	le Irlande (eerlaand)

Asia	l'Asie (aazee)
Africa	l'Afrique (aafreek)
Australia	l'Australie (ostraalee)
America	l'Amérique (aamereek)
Europe	l'Europe (urawp)

an American	un Américain (aamereeken)
a Frenchman	un Français (fraanse)
French language	Français
an Englishman	un Anglais (aangle)
English language	Anglais
a Swiss	un Suisse (swees)
a Japanese	un Japonais (zhaapawne)
a Russian	un Russe (ryus)
an Indian	un Hindou (endoo)
A Chinese	un Chinois (sheenwaa)

Before the name of countries the definite article 'le' is used.

'gn' is pronounced (ny).
'ai' has two sounds (ai), (e).

Lesson 26
Pronoun

<u>Personal Pronoun</u>

I	je (zhə)
we	nous (noo)
thou	tu (tyu)
you	vous (voo)
he	il (eel)
she	elle (el)
they (mas.)	ils (eel)
they (fem.)	elles (el)
it	ceci (sesee) / ce (sə)

<u>Possessive Pronoun</u>

my (mas.)	mon (mon)
	my father = mon père
	my teacher = mon maître (metr)
my (fem.)	ma (maa)
	my mother = ma mère
	my car = ma voiture (vwaatyur)
my (plu.)	mes (me / may)
	my brothers = mes frères
	my sisters = mes soeurs
our (m/f)	notre (notr)
	our frined = notre ami
our (plu.)	nos (no)
	our tickets = nos billets (beeye)
thy (m)	ton (ton)
	thy brother = ton frère
thy (f)	ta (taa)
	thy mother = ta mère
thy (plu)	tes (tay)
	thy pencils = tes crayons (kre-on)
your (m/f)	votre (votr)
	your table = votre table
your (plu)	vos (vo)
	your nephews = vos neveux
his/her (m)	son (son)
	his father = son père
	her father = son père

his/her (f)	sa (saa)
	his mother = sa mère
	her mother = sa mère
his/her (plu)	ses (se / say)
	his parents = ses parents
	her parents = ses parents
their (m/f)	leur (loer)
	their house = leur maison (mezon)
their (plu)	leurs (loer)
	their friends = leurs amis

Exception: - mon/son is used with the nouns starting with a, e, i, o, u even if the nouns are feminine.
my girlfriend (f) = mon amie
his school (f) = son école (ekawl)
my address (f) mon adresse (aadres)

<u>Objective Pronoun</u>

me	me (mə), moi (mwaa)
us	nous
thee	te (tə), toi (twaa)
you	vous
him	le, lui (lwee)
her	la, elle, lui
them	les, leur (loer)
it	le

<u>Interrogative Words</u>

what	quoi (kwaa)
who	qui (kee)
whom	que (kə)
whose	dont (dawn)
where	où (oo)
when	quand (kaan)
which	lequel (ləkel)
how	comment (kawmaan)
why	pour quoi (poor kwaa)
or	ou (oo)
otherwise	autrement (otremaan)
how much/many	combien (kawnbi-aan)

Note: - The sentences with these words will be given in next lessons because there other things that condition these words.

Teacher = professeure (prawfesoer), maître (metr).
The word 'On' (on) = someone. It is a pronoun which has indirect meaning = we, you, they, one.

Lesson 27
Present Tense

être (etr) = to be
The forms of the verb être in Present Tense

Affirmative
I am   = je suis (zhə swee)
Thou are   = tu es (tyu e)
He is   = il est (eel e)
She is   = elle est (el e)
We are   = nous sommes (noo sawm)
You are   = vous êtes (voozet)
They are (m)   = ils sont (eel sawn)
They are (f)   = elles sont (el sawn)
It is   = ce es (sə e)

Interrogative
Am I   = suis-je (swee zhə)
Are thou   = es-tu (e tyu)
Is he   = est-il (eteel)
Is she   = est-elle (etel)
Are we   = sommes-nous (sawm noo)
Are you   = êtes-vous (et voo)
Are they (m)   = sont-ils (sawn teel)
Are they (f)   = sont-elles (sawn tel)

Negative
I am not   = je ne suis pas (zhə nə swee paa)
Thou are not   = tu n'es pas (tyu nə paa)
He is not   = il n'est pas (eel nə paa)
She is not   = elle n'est pas (el nə paa)
We are not   = nous ne sommes pas (noo nə som paa)
You are not   = vous n'êtes pas (voo net paa)
They are not   = ils ne sont pas (eel nə son paa)
They are not   = elles ne sont pas (el nə son paa)

Interrogative Negative
Am I not   = ne suis-je pas (nə swee zhə paa)
Are thou not   = n'es-tu pas (ne tyu paa)
Is he not   = n'est-il pas (ne teel paa)
Is she not   = n'est-elle pas
Are we not   = ne sommes-nous pas
Are you not   = n'êtes-vous pas
Are they not   = ne sont-ils pas
Are they not   = ne sont-elles pas

Lesson 28

avoir (aavwaar) = to have

<u>Affirmative</u>

I have	= j'ai (zhai)
Thou have	= tu as (tyu aa)
He has	= il a (eel aa)
She has	= elle a (el aa)
We have	= nous avons (noozaavon)
You have	= vous avez (voozaave)
They have	= ils ont (eel zon)
They have	= elles ont (el zon)
It has	= ce a (sə aa)

<u>Interrogative</u>

Have I	= ai-je (ai zhə)
Have thou	= as-tu (aa tyu)
Has he	= a-t-il (aateel) *Extra 't' is to pronounce easily*
Has she	= a-t-elle (aatel)
Have we	= avons-nous (aavon noo)
Have you	= avez-vous (aave voo)
Have they	= ont-ils (on teel)
Have they	= ont-elles (on tel)

<u>Negative</u>

I have not	= je n'ai pas (zhə nai paa)
Thou have not	= tu n'as pas (tyu naa paa)
He has not	= il n'a pas (eel naa paa)
She has not	= elle n'a pas (el naa paa)
We have not	= nous n'avons pas (noo naavon paa)
You have not	= vous n'avez pas (voo naave paa)
They have not	= ils n'ont (eel non paa)
They have not	= elles n'ont (el non paa)

<u>Interrogative Negative</u>

Have I not	= n'ai-je pas (nai-zhə paa)
Have thou not	= n'as-tu pas (naa tyu paa)
Has he not	= n'a-t-il pas (naateel paa)
Has she not	= n'a-t- elle pas (naatel paa)
Have we not	= n'avons-nous pas (naavon noo paa)
Have you not	= n'avez-vous pas (naave voo paa)
Have they not	= n'ont-ils pas (nonteel paa)
Have they not	= n'ont-elles pas (nontel paa)

Hints:-

1. Have I = Do I have
2. French conjugation: – (Subject) + (Root of verb + ending) + (Object).
3. Syntax: - **I/he/she + root+e. Thou + root+es. We + root+ons. You + root+ez. They + root+ent.**

Lesson 29
Verbs

Each verb has several forms in Present, Past and Future Tense. It is hard to memorize all but proper understanding with mandatory practice is the way to get through it. In any dictionary of French you will find all the verb forms.

Here is a small list of verbs-

to have	= avoir (aavwaar)
to be	= être (etr)
to speak	= parler (paarle)
to eat	= manger (maanzhe)
to visit	= visiter (veezeete)
to read	= lire (leer)
to write	= écrire (ekreer)
to love	= aimer (eme)
to finish	= finir (feeneer)
to punish	= punir (pyuneer)
to wait	= attendre (aataandr)
to return	= rendre (raandr)
to know	= savoir (saavwaar)
to receive	= recevoir (resevwaar)
to ask	= demander (demaande)
to give	= donner (dawne)
to say/tell	= dire (deer)
to do/make	= faire (fer)
to see	= voir (vwaar)
to sell	= vendre (vaandr)
to insure	= assurer (aasyure)
to import	= importer (enpawrte)
to export	= exporter (ekspawrte)
to sign	= signer (seenye)
to request	= demander (demaande)
to consider	= compter (kawnte)
to drink	= boir (bwaar)
to sing	= chanter (shaante)
to go	= aller (aale)
to come	= venir (veneer)
to learn	= apprendre (aapraandr)
to teach	= enseigner (aansenye)
to take	= prendre (praandr)
to know	= connaître (kawnetr), savoir (səvwaar)
To buy	= acheter (aashete)

* Verbs ending with 'er' have 'r' silent.

Lesson 30
Present Indefinite Tense

aimer = to love
I love	= j'aime (zhaim)
Thou love	= tu aimes (tyu aim)
He loves	= il aime (eel aim)
She loves	= elle aime (el aim)
We love	= nous aimons (noozaimon)
You love	= vous aimez (voozaime)
They love	= ils/elles aiment (eel zaimaan)

parler = to speak
I speak	= je parle (zhə parl)
Thou speak	= tu parles (tyu parl)
He speaks	= il parle (eel parl)
She speaks	= elle parle (el parl)
We speak	= nous parlons (noo paarlon)
You speak	= vous parles (voo parle)
They speak	= ils/elles parlent (eel paarlaan)

finir = to finish
I finish	= je finis (zhə feenee)
Thou finish	= tu finis (tyu feenee)
He finishes	= il finit (eel feenee)
She finishes	= elle finit (el feenee)
We finish	= nous finissons (noo feeneeson)
You finish	= vous finissez (voo feeneese)
They finish	= ils / elles finissent (eel feeneesaan)

punir = to punish
I punish	= je punis (zhə pyunee)
Thou punish	= tu punis (tyu pyunee)
He punishes	= il punit (eel pyunee)
She punishes	= elle punit (el pyunee)
We punish	= nous punissons (noo pooneeson)
You punish	= vous punissez (voo pooneese)
They punish	= ils/elles punissent (eel pooneesaan)

attendre = to wait
I wait	= j'attends (zhaa-taan)
Thou wait	= tu attends (tyu aataan)
He waits	= il attend (eel aataan)
She waits	= elle attend (el aataan)
We wait	= nous attendons (noozaa-taandon)
You wait	= vous attendez (voozaa-taande)
They wait	= ils / elles attendent (eelzaataandaan)

rendre = to return

I return	= je rends (zhə raan)
Thou return	= tu rends (tyu raan)
He returns	= il rend (eel raan)
She returns	= elle rend (el raan)
We return	= nous rendons (noo raandon)
You return	= vous rendez (voo raande)
They return	= ils / elles rendent (eel raandaan)

From the above six examples of verbs in present tense, you may have noticed the three types of French verbs which end in –er, –ir and –re. We shall now summarize the rules with which the change in the verbs stem occurs in accordance with the subject.

The verbs ending in –er
1. With the subject 'I, he, she', the root (stem) of the verb takes additional –e, as:
aim+e | parl+e
In this, aimer is main verb, aim is root, and –e is additional.

2. With the subject 'thou', the root of the verb takes additional –es, as:
aim+es | parl+es

3. With the subject 'we', the root of the verb takes additional –ons, as:
aim+ons | parl+ons

4. With the subject 'you', the root of the verb takes additional –ez, as:
aim+ez | parl+ez

5. With the subject 'they', the root of the verb takes additional –ent, as:
aim+ent | parl+ent

The verbs ending in –ir
1. With the subject 'I, thou', the root of the verb takes additional –is, as:
fin+is | pun+is

2. With the subject 'he, she', the root of the verb takes additional –it, as:
fin+it | pun+it

3. With the subject 'we', the root of the verb takes additional –issons, as:
fin+issons | pun+issons

4. With 'you', the root takes additional –issez, as:
fin+issez | pun+issez

5. With 'they', the root takes additional –issent, as:
fin+issent | pun+issent

Do I speak	= Parle – je? / je parle? (old French) / est-ce-que je parle?
est-ce-que	= is it that?

The verbs ending in –re
1. With 'I, thou', the root takes additional –s, as:
attend+s | rend+s

2. With 'he, she', the root takes nothing as additional.
attend | rend

3. With 'we', the root takes additional –ons, as:
attend+ons | rend+ons

4. With 'you', the root takes additional –ez, as:
attend+ez | rend+ez

5. With 'they', the root takes additional –ent, as:
attend+ent | rend+ent

Now we take the fourth verb ending in –oir
savoir = to know / to understand
I know   = je sais (zhə sai)
Thou know   = tu sais (tyu sai)
He knows   = il sait (eel sai)
She knows   = elle sait (el sai)
We know   = nous savons (noo saavoη)
You know   = vous savez (voo saave)
They know   = ils / elles savent (eel saavann)

recevoir = to receive
I receive   = je reçois (zhə reswaa)
Thou receive   = tu reçois (tyu reswaa)
He receives   = il reçoit (eel reswaa)
She receives   = elle reçoit (el reswaa)
We receive   = nous recevons (noo resevoη)
You receive   = vous recevez (voo reseve)
They receive   = ils / elles reçoicent (eel reswaasaaη)

The verb ending in –oir is irregular kind of verb. The root of it takes –s for first person singular and –t for third person singular. The verbs ending in –er are almost 4,000 in French, –re are just 50, and –ir are about 300.

Exercise: -
Translate these sentences into French.

I speak. I do not speak. Do I speak? Do I not speak? He loves. He does not love. Does he love? Does he not love? You have. You do not have. Do you have? Do you not have? She is. She is not. Is she? Is she not? You are. We have. Thou speak. I love. We finish. He punishes. She waits. They return.

Lesson 31
Present Indefinite – Negative and Interrogative

As explained before, to make a negative sentence in French, put subject first, then 'ne', then verb, and lastly 'pas'. To make interrogative, put verb first, place a hyphen, and then put subject.

<u>First Person – 'I'</u>
To ask = demander (demaande) – root is 'demand'

I ask	= je demande (zhə demaand)
I do not ask	= je ne demande pas (zhə nə demand paa)
Do I ask	= demande-je (demaand zhə)

To give = donner (done) – root is 'donn'

I give	= je donne (zhə dawn)
I do not give	= je ne donne pas
Do I give	= donne-je

To say/tell = dire (deer) – root is 'di'

I say	= je dis (zhə dee)
I do not say	= je ne dis pas
Do I say	= dis-je

To read = lire (leer) – root is 'li'

I read	= je lis (zhə lee)
I do not read	= je ne lis pas
Do I read	= lis-je

To finish = finir (feeneer) – root is 'fin'

I finish	= je finis (zhə feenee)
I do not finish	= je ne finis pas
Do I finish	= finis-je

To punish = punir (pyuneer) – root is 'pun'

I punish	= je punis (zhə poonee)
I do not punish	= je ne punis pas
Do I punish	= punis-je

To speak = parler (paarle) – root is 'parl'

I speak	= je parle (zhə paarl)
I do not speak	= je ne parle pas
Do I speak	= parle-je

To do/make = faire (fayər) – root is 'fai'

I do	= je fais (zhə fai)
I do not do	= je ne fais pas
Do I do	= fais-je

To see = voir (voaar) – root is 'vo'
I see   = je vois (zhə vwaa)
I do not see   = je ne vois pas
Do I see   = vois-je

To sell = vendre (vaaɴdr) – root is 'vend'
I sell   = je vends (zhə vaaɴ)
I do not sell   = je ne vends pas
Do I sell   = vends-je

To go = aller (aale). It is an irregular verb with no root.
I go   = je vais (zhə vai)
I do not go   = je ne vais pas
Do I go   = vais-je

Note: - There are some irregular verbs which do not follow any rule. You can find out their forms in a
dictionary.

<u>Second and Third Person Singular</u>
He speaks   = il parle (il paarl)
He does not speak   = il ne parle pas
Does he speak   = parle-il?

Thou understand   = tu prends (tyu praaɴ)
Thou do not understand = tu ne prends pas
Do thou understand   = prends-tu?

<u>Plurals</u>
We begin   = nous commençons (komaaɴsoɴ)
We do not begin   = nous ne commençons pas
Do we begin   = commençons-nous

They laugh   = ils risent (eel reesaaɴ)
They do not laugh   = ils ne risent pas
Do they laugh   = risent-ils

Hints: - Living objective pronoun is always placed before a verb.
But non-living objective pronoun is placed after a verb.
I love you   = Je vous aim. / Je t'aime. (te (tə) = thee)
I know you   = Je vous connal.
I love music   = J'aime la musique.
I love you   = j'aime vous. (not okay)

Exercise: -
Translate these sentences into French.
I know. Thou do not know. Does he know? Does she not know? We wait. You do not wait. Do they wait?
She loves. I do not love? Does he love? Do you not love? Do we love? She punishes. Thou do not punish.
Do they punish? Do I not punish?

Lesson 32
Present Continuous Tense

In French, there is no present continuous tense. In stead of continuous, present indefinite tense is used.

I speak	= je parle
I am speaking	= je parle
He goes	= il va (vaa). ['va' is form of 'aller']
He is going	= il va
She eats	= elle mange (maaɴzh)
She is eating	= elle mange
We hear	= nous entendons (noo zaaɴtaaɴdoɴ)
We are hearing	= nous entendons
You do not speak	= nous ne parlez pas (parle)
You are not speaking	= nous ne parlez pas
Do they reply	= répondent-ils? (repawɴdaaɴ)
Are they replying	= répondent-ils?
Does he not sing	= ne chante-il pas? (shaaɴteel)
Is he not singing	= ne chante-il pas?

Note: - Generally with first person singular of –er verb, the use of inversion for forming interrogatives is avoided. In stead, 'est-ce-que' is used. Est-ce-que (eskə) = is it that.

Do I speak	= est-ce-que je parle?
Do I ask	= est-ce-que je demande?
Do I eat	= est-ce-que je mange?
Do I have	= est-ce-que j'ai?

The literal meaning of 'est-ce-que' is 'is this that.' So, in stead of 'Do I speak?' in French the sentence is framed like – 'Is it that I speak?' And it is applied with only first person singular. Though Interrogative Sentence Framing (as in English) doesn't exist in French, but you must use it to avoid ambiguity.

Exercise: -
Translate these sentences into French.

I know. I do not know. Do I know? Do I not know? He knows. He does not know. Does he know? Does he not know? We know. We do not know. Do we know? Do we not know? You know. You do not know. Do you know? Do you not know? They know. They do not know. Do they know? Do they not know? They are waiting. They are not waiting. Are they waiting? Are they not waiting? You are waiting. You are not waiting. Are you waiting? Are you not waiting? We are waiting. We are not waiting. Are we waiting? Are we not waiting? She is waiting. She is not waiting. Is she waiting? Is she not waiting? I am waiting. I am not waiting. Am I waiting? Am I not waiting?

Lesson 33
Present Prefect Tense

<u>Affirmative</u>

I have	= j'ai (zhai)
Thou have	= tu as (tyu aa)
He has	= il a (eel aa)
She has	= elle a (el aa)
We have	= nous avons (noozaavon)
You have	= vous avez (voozaave)
They have	= ils ont (il zon)
They have	= elles ont (el zon)
It has	= ce a (sə aa)

<u>Interrogative</u>

Have I	= ai-je (ai zhə)
Have thou	= as-tu (aa tyu)
Has he	= a-t-il (aateel)
Has she	= a-t-elle (aatel)
Have we	= avons-nous (aavon noo)
Have you	= avez-vous (aave voo)
Have they	= ont-ils (on teel)
Have they	= ont-elles (on tel)

<u>Negative</u>

I have not	= je n'ai pas (zhə nai paa)
Thou have not	= tu n'as pas (tyu naa paa)
He has not	= il n'a pas (eel naa paa)
She has not	= elle n'a pas (el naa paa)
We have not	= nous n'avons pas (noo naavons paa)
You have not	= vous n'avez pas (voo naave paa)
They have not	= ils n'ont (eel non paa)
They have not	= elles n'ont (el non paa)

<u>Interrogative Negative</u>

Have I not	= n'ai-je pas (nai zhə paa)
Have thou not	= n'as-tu pas (naa tyu paa)
Has he not	= n'a-t-il pas (naateel paa)
Has she not	= n'a-t- elle pas (naatel paa)
Have we not	= n'avons-nous pas (naavon noo paa)
Have you not	= n'avez-vous pas (naave voo paa)
Have they not	= n'ont-ils pas (nonteel paa)
Have they not	= n'ont-elles (nontel paa)

* Present Perfect tense also plays the role of Past Indicative tense (onetimer).

Past Participle Form

Rule 1
There is a past participle form of French verbs. In order to make it of –er ending verb, you have to remove 'r' and place an acute (') on e = é. It sounds (e) or (ei).
parler – parlé (parlay); visiter –visité (veeseetay) ; donner – donné (donay) ; aller – allé (aalay) ; arriver – arrivé (aareevay) ; aimer – aimé (aimay) ; demander – demandé (demaanday).

Sentences
I have spoken	= j'ai parlé (paarlei)
He has gone	= il a allé
We have given	= nous avons donné
You have visited	= vous avez visité
They have arrived	= elles ont arrivé

Rule 2
To make a past participle form of verbs ending in –ir, you have to remove 'r'.
finir – fini (feenee); punir – puni (pyuinee); applaudir [applaud] – applaudi ; venir – veni ; choisir (shwaazeer) [choose] – choisi ; sortir [go out] – sorti.

Sentences
I have finished	= j'ai fini
He has come	= il a veni
We have chosen	= nous avons choisi (shwaazee)
You have punished	= vous avez puni
They have gone out	= elles ont sorti

Rule 3
To make a past participle form of verbs ending in –re, you have to replace 're' with 'u'.
vendre [sell] – vendu (vaandyui) ; perdre [lose] – perdu ; battre [beat] – battu ; répondre – repondu ; lire – lu ; boire – bu ; croire [think] – cru.

Sentences
I have sold	= j'ai vendu (vaandu)
He has lost	= il a perdu
We have replied	= nous avons repondu (repondu)

Thus Past Participle or 'Regular' verbs are formed by replacing the endings as follow:
1. Verbs ending in –er are changed into é
2. Verbs ending in –ir are changed into i
3. Verbs ending in –re are changed into u

In the 'Irregular' verbs, the change is as follow:
avoir – eu ; être – été ; dire – dit ; faire –fait ; voir [see] – vu ; boire [drink] – bu.

Present Perfect – Negative

I have not spoken	= je n'ai pas parlé
He has not gone	= il n'a pas allé
We have not given	= nous n'avons pas donné
You have not visited	= vous n'avez pas visité
You have not punished	= vous n'avez pas puni
They have not gone out	= ils n'ont pas sorti
I have not finished	= je n'ai pas fini
He has not come	= il n'a pas veni

Present Perfect – Interrogative

Have we chosen	= avons nous choisi
Have they arrived	= ont elles arrivé
Have you punished	= avez vous puni
Have they gone out	= ont elles sorti
Have I sold	= ai je vendu
Has he lost	= a-t-il perdu
Have we replied	= avons nous repondu
Have I finished	= ai je fini

Past Indicative Tense

Past Indicative tense is a past onetimer tense. This tense does not independently exist in French but it is used as Present Perfect Tense.

I have spoken	= j'ai parlé
I spoke	= j'ai parlé

I have not spoken	= je n'ai pas parlé
I did not speak	= je n'ai pas parlé

Have I spoken	= ai je parlé
Did I speak	= ai je parlé

Exercise: -
Translate these sentences into French.

I speak French. I do not speak French. Do I speak French? Do I not speak French? You are going home [home = à la maison]. You are not going home. Are you going home? Are you not going home? She has eaten an apple [apple = une pomme]. She has not eaten an apple. Has she eaten an apple? Has she not eaten an apple? We sold a book. We did not sell a book. Did we sell a book? Did we not sell a book?

Lesson 34
Past Historic / Past Continuous

Past Historic is past multi-timer tense which also plays the role of Past Continuous tense. It describes the habitual action taken in past repeatedly.
For example: -
I used to speak = I was speaking
He used to play = He was playing

Rule 1
To make an historic form of verbs ending in –er or –re, you have to add the following to the stem:
With 'I' and 'thou – ais
With 'he' and 'she' – ait
With 'we'– ions
With 'you' – iez
With 'they' – aient

I used to give   = je donnais (don**ai**) *['ai' is heavier sound than 'e']*
I was giving   = je donnais

Thou used to give   = tu donnais (donai)
Thou were giving   = tu donnais

He/she used to give   = il donnait (donai)
He/she was giving   = il donnait

We used to give   = nous donnions (donio$n$)
We were giving   = nous donnions

You used to give   = vous donniez (doniye)
You were giving   = vous donniez

They used to give   = ils donnaient (donai-aa$n$)
They were giving   = ils donnaient

Rule 2
If the verbs are ending in –ir, you have to replace 'ir' with –issais.
I used to finish   = je finissais (feeneesai)
Exception
These rules are not applicable to the verb être. So the sentences are made like this:

être
I was   = je fus (fyu)
Thou were   = tu fus
He/she was   = il/elle fut (fyu)
We were   = nous fûmes (fyum)
You were   = vous fûtes (fyut)
They were   = ils/elles furent (fyuraa$n$)

Lesson 35
Past Perfect Tense

The sentences of this tense are formed using Initial Past + Past Participle Form. The Past Participle you have already leant in lesson 33. The following is used as Initial Past:

I had	= j'avais (zhaav**ai**) *It is 'ai' not 'e'*
Thou had	= tu avais
He/she had	= il/elle avait (aavai)
We had	= nous avions (noozaaveeon)
You had	= vous aviez (voozaavee-ye)
They had	= ils/elles avaient (eelzaa-vaiaan)

Complete Sentences

I had spoken	= j'avais parlé
Thou had spoken	= tu avais parlé
He/she had spoken	= il/elle avait parlé
We had spoken	= nous avions parlé
You had spoken	= vous aviez parlé
They had spoken	= ils/elles avaient parlé

I had gone	= j'avais allé
She had given	= elle-t-avait donné
We had arrived	= nous avions arrive
You had finished	= vous aviez fini
They had come	= ils avaient veni
He had beaten	= il avait battu
Thou had lost	= tu avais perdu
The man had seen	= l'homme avait vu
I had drunk	= j'avais bu
She had visited	= elle-t-avait visité
They had asked	= ils avaient demandé
We had chosen	= nous avions choisi
You had punished	= vous aviez puni
The father had gone	= le père avait allé
The woman had replied	= la femme avait repondu
The mother had applauded	= la mère avait applaudi
The brother had gone out	= le frère avait sorti
I had had	= j'avais eu
She had been	= elle-t-avait été

Past Indefinite tense can be devided in two tenses – 1. Past Indicative [onetimer] - (similar to Present Perfect). 2. Past Historic [multi-timer] - (similar to Past Continuous). In French, only three tenses are mostly used – Present Indefinite, Present Perfect, and Future Indefinite.

Exercise: -
Translate these sentences into French.
I have spoken. I had spoken. I have not spoken. I had not spoken. Have I spoken? Had I spoken? Have I not spoken? Had I not spoken? The man has spoken. The man had spoken.

Lesson 36
Future Indefinite Tense

There is a definite procedure for forming verbs in the future tense also.

1. With the subject 'I', the additional –ai is added to the complete verb without dropping anything.
I shall speak	= je parlerai (paarler**ai**)
I shall love	= j'aimerai (aimerai)
I shall visit	= je visiterai (viseeterai)
I shall finish	= je finirai (feeneerai)

2. With 'thou', we have to add –as in the complete verb.
Thou will speak	= tu parleras (paarleraa**)**
Thou will love	= tu aimeras (aimeraa)
Thou will receive	= tu recevras (resevraa)

3. With 'he' and 'she', we have to add –a in the complete verb.
He will speak	= il parlera (paarleraa)
She will love	= elle aimera (aimeraa)
He will play	= il répondra (repondraa)

4. With 'we', we have to add –ons in the complete verb.
We shall speak	= nous parlerons (paarleron)
We shall love	= nous aimerons
We shall finish	= nous finirons

5. With 'you', we have to add –ez in the complete verb.
You will speak	= vous parlerez (paarleray)
You will finish	= vous finirez
You will love	= vous aimerez

5. With 'they', we have to add –ont in the complete verb.
They will speak	= ils parleront (paarleron)
They will finish	= ils finiront (feeneeron)
They will love	= ils aimeront (aimeron)

The exceptional 'avoir' and 'être'
I shall have	= j'aurai (zhawrai)
Thou will have	= tu auras (awraa)
He/she will have	= il/elle aura
We shall have	= nous aurons (oron)
You will have	= vous aurez (oray)
They will have	= ils auront (awron)

I shall be	= je serai (serai)
Thou will be	= tu seras (seraa)
He/she will be	= il/elle sera (seraa)
We shall be	= nous serons (seron)
You will be	= vous serez (seray)
They will be	= ils seront (seron)

Exercise: -
Translate these sentences into French.

You visit. You do not visit. Do you visit? You are visiting. You are not visiting. Are you visiting? You have visited. You have not visited. Have you visited? You used to visit. You did not use to visit. Did you use to visit? You had visited. You had not visited. Had you visited? You will visit. You will not visit. Will you visit?

I eat.
You do not eat.
Does he eat?
You are speaking.
I am not speaking.
Is she speaking?
We have eaten.
They have not eaten.
Have thou eaten?
He used to love.
She did not use to love.
Did the man use to love?
The mother had gone.
The father had not gone.
Had the brother gone?
He will write.
You will not read.
Will we read?

Lesson 37
Some Expressions

Good morning = bonjour (bonzhoor)
Good evening = bonsoir (bonsoaar)
Good night = bonne nuit (bon nwee)
Good bye = au revoir (ore-vwaar)
Excuse me = excusez-moi (ekskyuze-mwaa)
Pardon me = pordonnez-moi
Yes, sir = oui, Monsieur (wee monsyu)
No, sir = non Monsieur (non)
Yes, miss = oui, Mademoiselle (mədmwaazel)
How are you madam? = comment allez-vous Madame? (kawmaan taale voo mədaam)
Fine, thanks, and you = très bien, merci, et vous (tre byaan, mersee, e voo)
No, thanks = non, merci (non)
Thank you very much = merci beaucoup (bokoo)
If you please = à votre grè. [grè = like] (à = aa)
You are very kind = vous êtes trop aimable (tropaimaabl)
Please = s'il vous plait (seel voo plai)
Sit down = asseyez-vous (eseye voo)
How is your family? = comment va votre famille? (faameeye) ['va' form of 'aller']
Very good = c'est parfait (se paarfai)
I congratulate you! = je vous felicite. (feleeseet) *<u>Object coming before verb</u>*
Oh, I am very sorry = oh, je regrette infiniment (regret enfeeneema)
Quite well! = très bien
It does not matter = n'importe (nenpawrte)
A happy journey! = bon voyage! (bon voyaazh)
I introduce you to my mother = je vous présente à ma mère (prezaan)
What is the matter with you? = qu'avez-vous? (kaave)
Leave me alone = laissez-moi tranquille (traankeel)
Help yourself = servez-vous
This will be easy = ce sera facile (faaseel)
Speak more slowly = parlez plus lentement (paarle plyu laantemaan)
Speak softly = parlez doucement (doosmaan)
That is all = c'est tout (se too)
That is to say = c'est à dire
Who is there? = qui est là? (kee – e – laa)
Whose car is that? = à qui est cettee auto? [à qui = to whom]
This book and that = ce livre et celui-là. [celui-là (selvee) = that one]
Don't speak = ne parlez pas
Who is there? = qui est là?
I am = moi (mwaa)
What is it? = qu'est-ce? (kes)
Would you like a cup of tea? = aimeriez-vous une tasse de thé?
I would like a glass of wine = j'aimerais un verre de vin (ver ven)
If you don't mind = si vous le voulez bien

Lesson 38
Introduction

My name is mark.
mon nom est Mark. (mon non)

I am thirty years old.
j'ai trente ans. (traant aan)

I live in Mumbai.
j'habite à Mumbai. (zhaabeet)

I am an Indian.
je suis un hindou. (endu)

Give me your address.
donnez-moi votre adresse.

I have a lot of work.
j'ai fort à faire. (fawr aa feər)

I need some money.
je nécessite l'argent. (neseseet laarzhaan)

My father is a doctor.
mon pére est le docteur. (dawktyur)

How glad I am to see you!
que je suis aise de vous voir! (aiz)

How is your family?
comment va votre famille?

I am very hungry / thirsty.
j'ai très faim / soif. (faan swaaf)

What is your name?
quel est votre nom?

Where do you live?
où habitez-vous? (aabite)

Have you seen my watch?
avez-vous vu ma montre? (vyu)

Yes, it is very nice.
oui, elle est trés jolie.

How much does this cost?
combien coute ceci? (kawbyaan koot sesee)

Do you like this country?
aimez-vous ce pays? (pe-i)

I am glad to see you.
je suis content de vous voir. (kontaan)

Where is the hotel?
où est l'hôtel?

The hotel is here.
l'hôtel est ici.

This will be your room.
ce sera votre chambre.

I wish to travel by plane.
je voudrais allez en avion. [en = in] (voodrai aan aavyon)

Everything is ready.
tout est prêt. (too e pre)

What is your telephone number?
quel est votre numéro de telephone? (kel numero də telefon)

My number is.
mon numéro est.

I want to telephone.
je desire téléphoner. (dezeer telephone)

There is a phone call for you.
il y un coup de telephone pour vous. [il y = there is] (eel ee koo)

Call the doctor.
faites venir le médecin. (faite veneer medesen)

How is the weather?
quel temps fait-il? (taan faiteel)

It is going to rain.
il va pleuvoir. (pluvwaar)

There is a big difference between your climate and ours.
il y une grosse différence entre votre climat et la nôtre. (eel ee deeferaans aantr kleema)

Lesson 39
Modal Verbs **Verbs modaux** (verb mawdu)

pouvoir (poovwaar) = can (to be able to), may
Je peux aller à l'école.
I can go to (the) school.
Nous pouvons parler français.
We can speak French.

pourrait (poorai) = could (was able to)
Je ne pu pas écrire de letter.
I could not (was not able to) write a letter.
Ils ne pouvaient pas parler français.
They could not speak French.

devoir (devwaar) = should (to be bound to), have to, must
Tu dois chanter une chanson.
Thou (you) should sing a song.
Nous devons acheter des livres.
We should buy books.

voudrais (voodrai) = would (past of will = vouloir)
Elle mangerait des pommes.
She would eat apples.
Elle mangera des pommes.
She **will** eat apples.

Vous conduiriez une voiture.
You would drive a car.
Vous conduirez une voiture.
You **will** drive a car.

passé devoir = had to
Nous devions attendre.
We had to wait.
Il devait gagner de l'argent.
He had to earn money.

Hints: -
He used to play. = He played.
I can go. = I may go.

Lesson 40

Soi - introduction Self-Introduction

My name is Niranjan Showman.
Je m'appelle Niranjan Showman.

I live in Mumbai, India.
Je vis à Bombay, en Inde.

My job is teaching languages.
Mon travail est l'enseignement des langues.

I have written some books.
J'ai écrit quelques livres.

I like to read books and watch movies.
J'aime lire des livres et regarder des films.

My city is beautiful and rich.
Ma ville est belle et riche.

I have two brothers and no sister.
J'ai deux frères et pas de soeur.

I am thirty-five years old.
J'ai trente-cinq ans.

I can speak English and French.
Je peux parler anglais et français.

My hobby is to visit new places.
Mon hobby est de visiter de nouveaux endroits.

Now I want to visit Europe.
Maintenant, je veux visiter l'Europe.

Speaking a foreign language is good for my career.
Parler une langue étrangère est bon pour ma carrière.

Europeans are great discoverers.
Les Européens sont de grands découvreurs.

Thank you.
Merci.

Lesson 41

Ma ville Mumbai My city Mumbai

Mumbai is a big city of India.
Mumbai est une grande ville de l'Inde.

It is the financial capital of the country.
C'est la capitale financière du pays.

I live in this city from twenty years.
Je vis dans cette ville depuis vingt ans.

Mumbai is thickly populated.
Mumbai est densément peuplée.

People have very busy life here.
Les gens ont une vie très occupée ici.

Mumbai is famous for film production.
Mumbai est célèbre pour la production cinématographique.

Many film stars live here.
De nombreuses stars de cinéma vivent ici.

Life is very expensive for all.
La vie est très chère pour tous.

There are many beautiful places here.
Il y a beaucoup de beaux endroits ici.

Local train is life-line of this city.
Le train local est la ligne de vie de cette ville.

I like this for its beauty.
J'aime ça pour sa beauté.

I live here for prosperity.
Je vis ici pour la prospérité.

Mumbai is a cosmopolitan cit.
Mumbai est une ville cosmopolite.

I like this city for weather.
J'aime cette ville pour le temps.
Thank you.
Merci.

Lesson 42

Notre pays Inde Our country India

India is my country.
L'Inde est mon pays.
I am an Indian citizen.
Je suis citoyen indien.

Our country is in Asian continent.
Notre pays est sur le continent asiatique.

Our national language is Hindi.
Notre langue nationale est l'hindi.

We have our national flag.
Nous avons notre drapeau national.

Hockey is our national sport.
Le hockey est notre sport national.

Tiger is our national animal.
Le tigre est notre animal national.

There are many rivers in India.
Il existe de nombreuses rivières en Inde.

This is the seventh largest country of the world.
C'est le septième plus grand pays du monde.

India is a secular democratic country.
L'Inde est un pays démocratique laïc.

We have New Delhi as capital.
Nous avons New Delhi comme capitale.

We believe in peace and prosperity.
Nous croyons en la paix et la prospérité.

India is an agricultural region.
L'Inde est une région agricole.
It has many beautiful places to visit.
Il a beaucoup de beaux endroits à visiter.

India has very nice weather.
L'Inde a un temps très agréable.
I love my country.
J'aime mon pays.

Lesson 43

Sur la France About France

France is a country in Europe.
La France est un pays d'Europe.

Its neighbors are Germany, Italy and Belgium.
Ses voisins sont l'Allemagne, l'Italie et la Belgique.

Paris is the capital of France.
Paris est la capitale de la France.

It is also a beautiful city.
C'est aussi une belle ville.

It is the most populated city of the country.
C'est la ville la plus peuplée du pays.

French is the national language of France.
Le français est la langue nationale de la France.

This country has eighteen regions.
Ce pays compte dix-huit régions.

The total population is sixty-seven million.
La population totale est de soixante-sept millions.

Marseille is the second largest city.
Marseille est la deuxième plus grande ville.

It has the biggest port in France.
Elle possède le plus grand port de France.

French culture is more than two thousand year old.
La culture française a plus de deux mille ans.

French cooking is superb to mankind.
La cuisine française est superbe pour l'humanité.

Thank you.
French: Merci.

Writing this book was really challenging to me.
I thank you for learning this much!
As you have reached here, now you need a French to English dictionary.
Start reading the SIMPLE text of French or refer to my next book "Foreign Languages Conversation".
If required, now you can do French A1 certified course and ask us the detail.
Reading simple stories and watching videos will also be a great help.
Daily practice on what you have learnt is necessary to stop from falling down.
Expand your reach with confidence and enter the world of French with gradual and continuous move.
Reading, writing, speaking and listening –do all the four things until you find yourself fully strengthened.
To do French A1 course, you can cantact us for further learning.
You have to pass DELF A1 examination for French A1 level.

Niranjan Jha Showman
Trainer, Author, Physician, Entrepreneur, Filmmaker, Activist
Founder of Cromosys Corporation
facebook.com/cromosys
+91-9561450045
cromosys@yahoo.com
Nallasopara (W), Mumbai, India

Communicate with People

Listen to Them Carefully

Engage in Conversation

Develop Your Style

Read As Much As Possible

Speak Confidently

NIRANJAN JHA SHOWMAN

Cromosys Publication
Teach
Yourself
German
NIRANJAN JHA SHOWMAN

Cromosys Publication
Teach
Yourself
French
NIRANJAN JHA SHOWMAN

Cromosys Publication
Teach
Yourself
Spanish
NIRANJAN JHA SHOWMAN

Cromosys Publication

English Voice Accent and Pronunciation

NIRANJAN JHA SHOWMAN

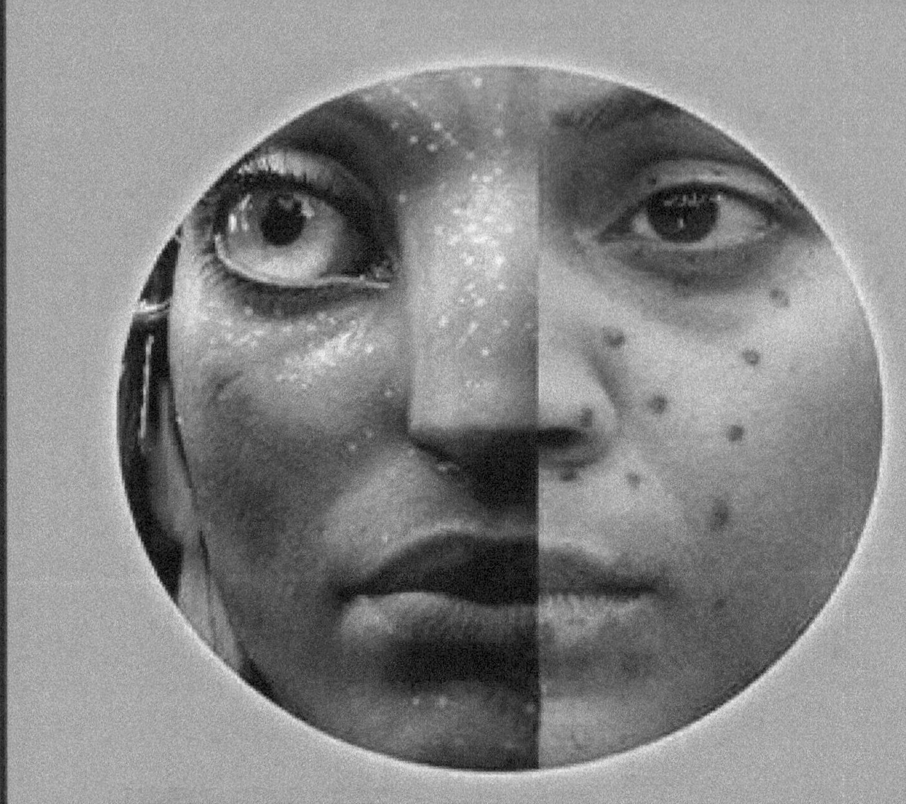

Teach
Yourself
Autodesk
MAYA

Cromosys Publication

NIRANJAN JHA SHOWMAN

Cromosys Publication
Teach
Yourself
Autodesk
3ds Max
NIRANJAN JHA SHOWMAN

Cromosys Publication
CRIMINAL FACTORY
NIRANJAN JHA SHOWMAN

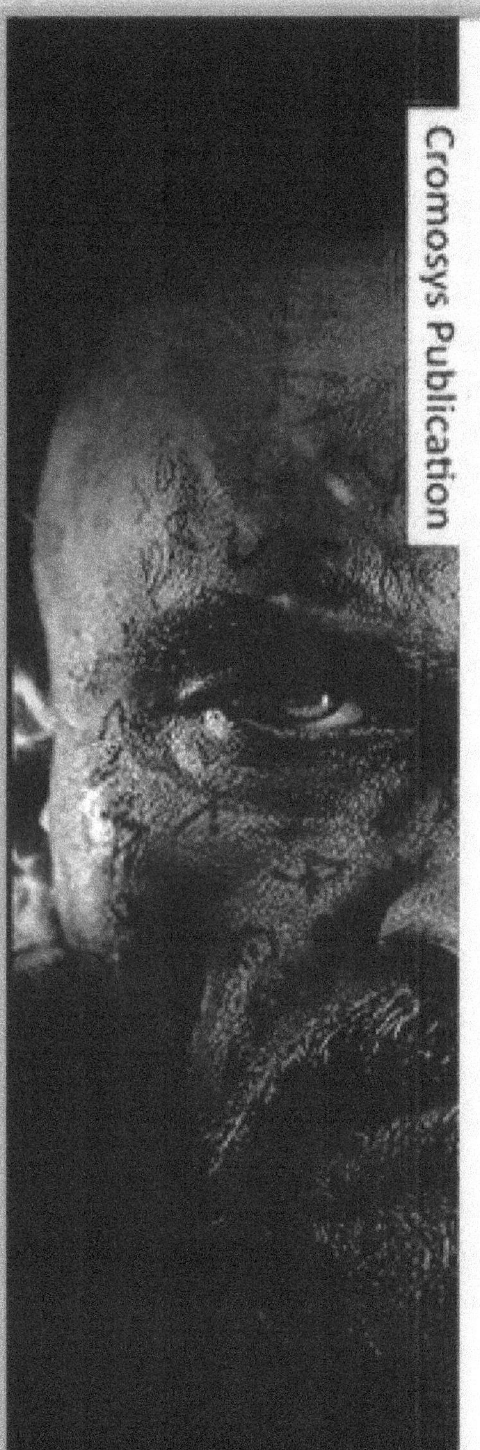

Cromosys Publication
FOCAL DISASTER
NIRANJAN JHA SHOWMAN

Cromosys Publication
Your talents will not help you succeed without your skill of using them.
NIRANJAN JHA SHOWMAN
BE
MILLIONAIRE
LIKE
ME

Copyright Office
Government of India

सत्यमेव जयते

Extracts
from the Register
of Copyrights

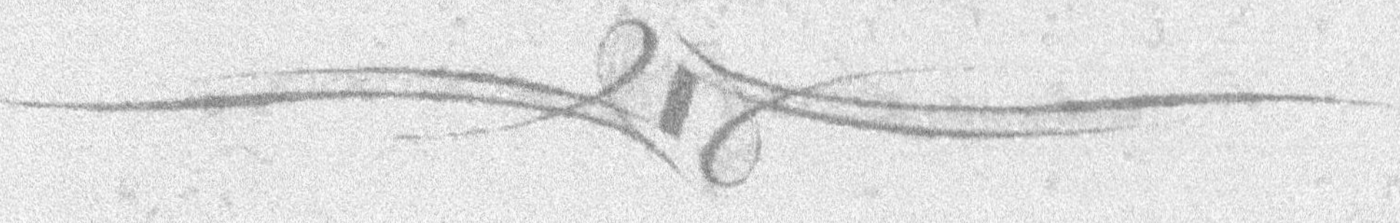

Dated : 24/07/2022

1.	Registration Number	: **N-76768/2022**
2.	Name, address and nationality of the applicant	: NIRANJAN JHA SHOWMAN, CROMOSYS PUBLICATION, 001, JAYSATYAM, PATANKAR ROAD, NALLASOPARA (W), MUMBAI, MAHARASHTRA - 401203. INDIAN
3.	Nature of the applicant's interest in the copyright of the work	: AUTHOR
4.	Class and description of the work	: LITERARY / BOOK
5.	Title of the work	: TEACH YOURSELF FRENCH
6.	Language of the work	: ENGLISH
7.	Name, address and nationality of the author and if the author is deceased, date of his decease	: NIRANJAN JHA SHOWMAN, CROMOSYS PUBLICATION, 001, JAYSATYAM, PATANKAR ROAD, NALLASOPARA (W), MUMBAI, MAHARASHTRA - 401203. INDIAN
8.	Whether the work is published or unpublished	: UNPUBLISHED
9.	Year and country of first publication and name, address and nationality of the publisher	: N.A.
10.	Years and countries of subsequent publications, if any, and names, addresses and nationalities of the publishers	: N.A. SAME AS ABOVE
11.	Names, addresses and nationalities of the owners of various rights comprising the copyright in the work and the extent of rights held by each, together with particulars of assignments and licences, if any	:
12.	Names, addresses and nationalities of other persons, if any, authorised to assign or licence of rights comprising the copyright	: N.A.
13.	If the work is an 'Artistic work', the location of the original work, including name, address and nationality of the person in possession of the work. (In the case of an architectural work, the year of completion of the work should also be shown).	: N.A.
14.	If the work is an 'Artistic work', whether it is registered under the Designs Act 2000 if yes give details.	: N.A.
15.	If the work is an 'Artistic work', capable of being registered as a design under the Designs Act 2000.whether it has been applied to an article though an industrial process and ,if yes ,the number of times it is reproduced.	: N.A.
16.	Remarks, if any	:

Diary Number :   7396/2020-CO/N
Date of Application :   09/05/2020
Date of Receipt :   09/05/2020

DEPUTY REGISTRAR OF COPYRIGHTS